Eastern National Parks

CLB 1970
© 1990 Colour Library Books Ltd., Godalming, Surrey, England.
All rights reserved.
This 1990 edition published by Crescent Books,
distributed by Outlet Book Company, Inc., a Random House Company,
225 Park Avenue South, New York, New York 10003.
Printed and bound in Italy.
ISBN 0 517 64417 7
8 7 6 5 4 3 2 1

Eastern National Parks

James V. Murfin

Introduction by Bill Harris

CRESCENT BOOKS
NEW YORK

Introduction
by Bill Harris

If there are 10,000 lakes in Minnesota, it would be easy to imagine that every one of them is in Voyageurs National Park. Of the 340 square miles of wilderness it contains, 130 miles of them are covered with water, and one of the big lakes is cut in half by the Canadian border. By Minnesota standards that's an average ratio, but by National Park standards it's probably the wettest in the system except for the Everglades in Florida, which is really a slow-moving river that covers more than 2,000 square miles.

The 17th century French trappers who called themselves voyageurs would recognize the waterscapes and landscapes in the park that was named for them. Spruce trees and firs still fill the air with their fragrance and still give shelter to black bears and moose. The waterways still provide hunting for bald eagles and hawks and shelter for mink and otter. Except for the smaller Isle Royale National Park, an island off the coast of Michigan in Lake Superior, it is the only National Park that has such spectacular virgin forests and waterways. Both Parks are covered with thick forests and both are the only National Parks south of the Canadian border with resident wolf packs within their boundaries. The wolves of Isle Royale apparently arrived over the frozen lake in winter. Man is forced to make the journey by boat or float plane, and as a result there are no roads or automobiles on the 45-mile long island.

Automobiles add to the joy of visiting Shenandoah National Park in the Blue Ridge Mountains of Virginia. The rolling hills and valleys are best seen from the 105-mile Skyline Drive, which also provides access to hiking trails for people who would rather have the adventure of an encounter with a whitetail deer, or watch the spring bird migration from a wildflower-strewn meadow. But, for the car-bound, the trip has just begun when the Skyline Drive ends at Rockfish Gap and joins the Blue Ridge Parkway, a 469-mile route across the spine of the Blue Ridge to North Carolina and Great Smoky Mountains National Park. If there is a more beautiful highway in the Eastern United States, it certainly doesn't have a more beautiful destination than the hardwood forest straddling North Carolina and Tennessee. There are more than 130 kinds of trees in Great Smoky Mountains National Park, and clusters of rhododendrons that grow as tall as 20 feet and bloom well into the summer. It's a place where you can make friends with a wild turkey or keep your distance from a bobcat, or just enjoy the most majestic of the National Parks east of Yellowstone.

There is majesty of a different sort up in Kentucky at Mammoth Cave National Park, where more than 300 miles of caverns on five levels include underground lakes, rivers and waterfalls. Above ground there are more than 200 species of birds in a hardwood forest that is a joy to behold in the fall when the leaves turn color. But it's what's below ground that visitors go there to see, and no one goes away disappointed. The limestone formations range from delicate, flower-like forms to a massive flowstone that lives up to its name as a Frozen Niagara.

It's chilly down there all the time, but Hot Springs National Park in Arkansas has plenty of evidence that not everything below the surface is cold. The water that comes out of the ground can be as hot as 150 degrees. The mineral springs, which some people believe have the power to cure almost anything that ails them, are what lure visitors there. Even if they're wrong, very few of them ever regret the experience. The wilderness experience at Hot Springs isn't the same as at other National Parks, but there is no rule that says all National Parks have to be the same.

The one that's completely different from all the others is Everglades Park in Southern Florida. There are trees and air plants, ferns and flowers there that don't exist anywhere else in the United States. There are birds, like spoonbills and types of egrets, that don't fly anywhere else. And where else would you expect a crocodile sanctuary?

Everglades Park is about as far South as it is possible to go on the East Coast of the United States. About as far North as you can go is another kind of National Park, Acadia on the coast of Maine. It covers some 60 square miles, including the beautiful Mount Desert Island with its 1,500-foot Mount Cadillac. It is a sanctuary for a vastly different kind of wildlife and plantlife than the Everglades and includes mountains and lakes, forests and ocean vistas that are more what people expect when they think of a National Park.

But one of the glories of the American National Park system is that no two of the Parks are exactly alike. Each of them is unique, each a source of inspiration. And until you've seen all of them, it's safe to say "you ain't seen nothing yet!"

1

Voyageurs National Park

Be it enacted by the Senate and House of Representatives of the United States of America in Congress Assembled:
That the purpose of this Act is to preserve, for the inspiration and enjoyment of present and future generations, the
outstanding scenery, geological conditions and waterway systems which constituted a part of the Voyageurs who
contributed to the opening of the Northwestern United States.
Public Law 91-662, January 8, 1971

The histories of Rocky Mountain, Grand Teton, and Yellowstone National Parks hint at the fur trade of the eighteenth and early nineteenth centuries that brought a unique breed of man into this vast wilderness looking for the beaver and sent him home filled with tales of wonder. Their stories are more often than not shadowed by what they found – the mountains, rivers, glaciers and other geological phenomena that, in most cases, were merely barriers.

Here is a national park, however, that not only encompasses within its boundaries some of the very land where trappers plied their trade, but honors the profession by name: Voyageurs National Park.

It is, of course, much more than a monument to an important chapter of American history, for the things associated with these extraordinary frontiersmen – the forts and trails – have long since vanished. But the lakes and forests they traveled have been little disturbed, and here in Northern Minnesota, just east of International Falls and along the Canadian border, are 219,000 acres of pristine North Woods – fir, spruce, pine, aspen, and birch – as they saw them.

Surely men explored North America because that was the nature of the pioneers who, no sooner landing on the Eastern shores, moved toward the West in search of land and food. Timber, gold, and a dozen other attractions drew them, acre by acre, mile by mile, into the frontiers. But the North American beaver, probably more than any other single factor in those early days, was responsible for the gradual exploration of the North Country.

Back in Europe, where the whims of fashion had already changed the course of history many times, one more, the beaver hat, set in motion the conquering of a land, wars between nations, and the beginning of an industry that still thrives. A beaver hat was a prized possession in the 1600s, a sign of wealth and high social status. But the European beaver was small and its fur was no match for the large pelts found in North America. The first traders, who explored what is now Minnesota, returned to England in 1666 with furs worth $100,000. They had found America's first gold, and for the next 200 years they mined it methodically and with a passion.

First there was the trader or the trading company – and trading it was, for there were no cash transactions on this side of the Atlantic. The trader

bought items in Europe – knives, mirrors, pots, needles, wine – that were negotiable with the trappers. The trapper furnished the beaver pelts in exchange. Now we come to the voyageur. He was the middleman, so to speak. The voyageur carried the merchandise to the trading posts in the wilderness and returned with the furs. Today this is a simple matter, but it took a special kind of human being in the eighteenth and nineteenth centuries to be a voyageur, and that's what this park is all about.

At first the Indians came to the trader-trade fairs at Montreal and Quebec. As competition increased and hostilities grew between tribes, and the "beaver frontier" pushed back, the trader began intercepting the trapper in the wilds. Soon the pattern reversed, and the trader was going virtually to the traps himself.

Voyageur is French for "traveler," a man who could survive the most strenuous journeys through the uncharted forests, streams and rivers of the North Country, paddling canoes, carrying supplies, and coping with rigorous weather conditions. He was French-Canadian, short (about five feet, six inches), rugged, and a member of what became a very elite society. There were two voyageurs: those who traveled west with the merchandise, and those who lived in the wilderness and dealt with the Indians and then trekked from the Northwest trapping outposts eastward. They met at Grand Portage on the shores of Lake Superior.

What made these people so special was their

inordinate strength and endurance. They traveled thousands of miles by canoe, some thirty-five feet long, with a crew of twelve, and carried their cargoes hundreds of miles overland at portages. A trip west from Montreal began as soon as the river ice melted and ended at Grand Portage in July. The return trip would take them home just before the ice set in again. At the other end of the line the voyageurs carried the beaver pelts by land and water equal distances to the exchange point and then returned before the early autumn snows. It was a hard life that went on for generations.

The fur trade ended in the mid-nineteenth century, when fashions throughout the world changed. Silk became the "in" thing and the demand for beaver fur dropped dramatically. And none too soon. No real attempt had been made to repopulate the beaver; it nearly became extinct. And so did the voyageur. Washington Irving wrote of them:

"Their glory is departed. They are no longer lords of our internal seas and the great navigators of the wilderness. Some of them may still occasionally be seen coasting the lower lakes with their frail barks, and pitching their camps and lighting their fires upon the shore; but their range is fast contracting to those remote waters and shallow, obstructed rivers unvisited by the steamboats. In the course of years they will gradually disappear; their songs will die away like the echoes they once awakened, and the Canadian voyageurs will become a forgotten race, or remembered, like their associates, the Indians, among the poetical images of past time, and as themes for local and romantic associations."

Perhaps the gutsy, fun-loving, and industrious voyageur has finally found his place in history, but, one might ask, why romanticize an industry that so blatantly destroyed native wildlife? The Congressional Act preserves "the outstanding scenery, geological conditions, and waterway system which constituted a part of the historic route of the Voyageurs...," 219,000 acres, about 85,000 of which are water and all the rest heavily forested. Much of the land is undeveloped and accessible only by motorboat and is, in our parlance, one of those last vestiges of wilderness-America, a microcosm, in effect, of the whole northern region of the country and of the route traveled by the voyageur.

This splendid, unspoiled land is built on the most solid foundation – ancient Precambrian rock laid down billions of years ago and shaved off by giant glaciers. It is a land like no other, interwoven by waterways, lakes of all sizes and shapes, islands big and small, framed by great vertical cliffs and huge boulders dropped by the melting ice of forgotten times. One senses the strong arm of Hiawatha, moccasins of deerskin, birch-bark canoes, the wigwam of Nokomis... a lonely silence broken only by the occasional dip of a paddle or the scream of a soaring eagle.

Voyageurs National Park was established in 1975 and is still being developed as a full-scale park. The first major development in the park, the Rainy Lake Visitor Center, opened in 1987. Other visitor facilities are located at Kabetogama, Ash River and Crane Lake, which are the access points into the park.

Over one hundred primitive, boat-in campsites dot the park's islands and shorelines. Private campgrounds and resorts are located around the perimeter of the park.

Hiking the Cruiser Lake Trail is one of the best ways to experience the moods and faces of the park. The 10-mile trail traverses the Kabetogama peninsula. The park's newest trail, the Locator Lake

Above: the showy lady's slipper peeps between cool tongues of greenery, and (facing page) a crimson sunset floods the Kabetogama Narrows. (National Park Service Photos by Dan Ritter.)

Nature Trail, offers some of the finest vistas in the park. Summer and winter trails continue to be developed throughout the park.

Voyageurs offers visitors a chance to explore the natural environment and the history of Minnesota's northwoods residents with a National Park Service naturalist. A wide variety of naturalist-guided boat trips, hikes and programs are offered during the summer.

Everything one could possibly want is here, however, and in these times it is all anyone really needs – a nature as refreshing as the spirit of the adventurer who, with but the fibers of birch bark and the determination to survive, molded an empire and opened a highway into the wilderness.

Sigurd Olson wrote in his *Reflections from the North Country:*

"It is good for us to recall the hardihood and simplicities that period represents, for we are still part of those frontiers and will survive because of what they gave us. We must solve the enormous problems that confront us, far bigger ones than we have ever known, but we face them with those sterling qualities woven into our pioneer character. Within us is an inner reserve of power and resilience because of what the frontiers did."

2
Isle Royale National Park

To step into Isle Royale is to leave behind one's old self and one's old world and to begin a new exploration into the nature of life.
Napier Shelton, *The Life of Isle Royale*

No doubt there are those who flinch at the association of wolf-moose, prey-predator relationship with Isle Royale National Park, so overworked and overtold is the story. Yet it is, in the words of Michael Frome, "a dramatic national park saga."

Rather than so often studying the cause of wildlife extinction, scientists' seeming misfortune, here on Isle Royale man has witnessed in modern times an evolution of migration, growth and dissipation and behavioral habits of two native North American mammals. The island is a laboratory.

This marvelous wilderness sanctuary lies just fifteen miles off Canada, in Lake Superior. Its close proximity to the mainland, yet its isolation and size – forty-five miles long, nine miles wide – has made it just right for a microcosm of nature's balance – neat and compact for a close look.

A 1905 Michigan Biological Survey of Isle Royale (the island is within the boundaries of Michigan) shows not a single moose on the island – lots of other wildlife, but no moose – nor can a wolf be found listed. Sometime after 1905, some think the winter of 1912, when the lake froze, a family of moose wandered across the ice. Within a short time the population had doubled, and so on, and so on, until the mid-thirties, when some three thousand were literally starving to death. There simply was not enough browse, or food, to sustain a herd this size. Many died in 1933, and in 1936, when fire burned a quarter of the island; the herd dropped to four hundred.

Vegetation soon renewed and also the moose, until about 1948, when another of those mysterious and unseen things happened that aided nature in its "perfect balance." Lake Superior froze again, and this time the wolf came to the island for the first time. The prey-predator relationship among wildlife took on a new dimension. The wolves, only about twenty or so, now keep the moose herd at just the right level to survive, and nearly every phase of the behavior of these two animals is studied with care. They both thrive in the most ideal conditions. And so does man.

Isle Royale National Park is a rock fortress, capped by dense forests and peppered, it seems, with lakes, streams, and hundreds of little off-shore islands. It has been called the nearest thing to a true wilderness we have outside of Alaska, but it has not by any means missed the world of man. There was a time, before it became a park in 1940, when human ramblings took their toll.

During the beaver-trapping days of the voyageurs there were six trading posts here; the Hudson's Bay

Above: wolves feeding on the carcass of a moose. Facing page: (bottom) Isle Royale's autumnal beauty, and (top) the melancholy loveliness of Tobin Harbor, presenting the gentler faces of the park .

Company had one or two, the others belonging to the American Fur Company. In the nineteenth century copper mining brought hundreds from the mainlands, Canada, and Michigan; hundreds who simply followed the footsteps of early natives whose open pits gave clues to the element found nowhere else around this country. Much of the virgin forest was burned away to expose the precious metal. But, as with the wildlife, the wilderness has sought its balance, and the island today is much as it was when first discovered.

The foundation of Isle Royale is lava dating back some 1.2 million years, layers of lava flows that tilted and dipped at angles. It is the gentle peaks of these strata, jutting upwards through the lake, that form the island. Glacial ice – billions of tons of it – depressed most of this, but as the ice melted and land rebounded, so to speak, Isle Royale began to "emerge." It continues to do so at the rate of about a foot or more each century. Here and there can be seen previous shorelines marked by gravel and smooth, rounded stones.

This is just one of the fascinating mysteries cloaked by the isolation of this quiet place in the north country. Isle Royale is one of nature's artifacts, large enough to be a haven for those who seek solitude under most primitive conditions, small enough to be seen as a living tool in understanding life itself.

3
Acadia National Park

Acadia ... where can you find anything in our country to match these mountains that come down to the ocean, these granite cliffs alongside which the biggest ships could ride, these bays dotted with lovely islets clothed in hardwood and hemlock, altogether such a sweep of rugged coastline as has no parallel from Florida to the Canadian provinces? ... Everything is here to rejoice the soul of the human visitor.
Freeman Tilden, *The National Parks*

Early one autumn morning during World War II, it is said, a German submarine slipped quietly into Frenchman Bay, past Bar Harbor on Mount Desert Island and, someplace in the deep waters along this Maine coastline, set three spies off in a rubber raft toward the rocky shore. The story is apocryphal; but if a U-boat commander did venture into this harbor, he knew exactly what he was doing. The waters along Maine's coast are deep; Somes Sound, which penetrates Mount Desert Island, is a fjord that is at once inviting and yet hostile in welcome.

Sunrise touches the United States first here at Acadia National Park in Maine, a place where, in contrast to the delicate morning light and the surrounding soft fingers of fog, the irresistible sea clashes harshly with an immovable, rocky coastline. By comparison, Acadia is one of the smaller national parks, but its size makes it no less important in the chain of great natural areas held in preservation by the nation. As a matter of fact, it is the size that makes it such a special place: the last vestige of the "rock-bound coast of Maine." There is really nothing quite like it along the Atlantic, and no other place in the East where the geological story is so closely linked to glaciers and the sea. Nor is there another park on this coast where the forces of nature are so blatantly obvious.

From about Portland to the St. Croix River, which separates Maine from New Brunswick - perhaps 185 miles as the crow flies - there are some 2,500 tortuous miles of jagged shoreline: inlets, coves, bays and sounds of fortress-like granite cliffs and boulder-strewn beaches. Only a small part of this is Acadia: Mount Desert Island, Isle au Haut, and the tip of Schoodic Peninsula - some 35,000 acres in all. But nature's relentless shaping, defining, and redefining of this land is nowhere better demonstrated than right here.

Scientists speculate that Acadia had several lives before the great Ice Age; times when it was covered by the sea; times much warmer when lava flowed and the land was molded into mountains and valleys; times when the rocks were formed and trees grew and even life itself began to crawl and fly about. It was the time of gigantic glaciers, however, that created most of what we see today - glaciers of about twenty five thousand years ago. That's almost like yesterday on the geological clock.

It was in 1837 that Swiss naturalist Louis Agassiz first talked about glaciers covering northern Europe. When he came to this country and saw Mount Desert Island in 1846, he soon made comparisons and announced that America, too, had once been covered with ice, and that it may have been glaciers nine thousand feet think that had carved this coastline. In fact, we now believe the glaciers to have been approximately 3,000 feet thick. Nevertheless, Agassiz's theories were startlingly accurate.

At one time the coast of this area was considerably farther out to sea. Glaciers from the north carved much of it away, and as the ice melted and the sea rose, what were once river valleys and stream beds were filled by the ocean, and mountain tops became islands. In essence, the weight of the ice (a single acre, one mile thick, may have weighed seven million tons) and its constant movement depressed and wore down the land and carried the debris to the sea. As the ocean moved in, it literally drowned the coast. And today, in a never-ending geologic evolution, the sea and the

Set amid the chiseled granite cliffs, Bass Harbor Head Light (below) is a welcoming sentinel to mariners when fog hides the dangerous coastline.

Above: behind the golden tints of fall foliage nestle the Hamilton Laboratory Farm Buildings.

land continue their battle – enormous energy unleashed in tides that batter and carve and change.

At Thunder Hole, for example, rushing tides lash at a narrow chasm of rock with mighty, near-sonic booms, trying desperately, it seems, to claim even more of the land. Huge boulders torn away by the sea are thrown back like pebbles. At Baker Island giant slabs of granite are cracked and ripped away as if by some powerful machine and carried away, only to be flung back to rebuild the shoreline somewhere else.

Lest Acadia be imagined a place of violence, a walk only yards from the shore will quickly dispel that. The land is hospitable, pristine, and often within only a step or tree-trunk from the lofty geysers created by the tides.

First established as Sieur de Monts National Monument in 1916, then Lafayette National Park in 1919, Acadia, renamed in 1929, was the first national park in the east and the only one in New England. Most of the park is on Mount Desert Island, where for many years the property was owned by "summer residents." It was this group of people, bent on protecting the wilderness, that created the park by giving their land to the federal government. The boundaries are as jagged as the shore, but this is a park that has grown and developed from within. Cadillac Mountain, 1,530 feet, is the highest point on the Atlantic coast. Below it lies Frenchman Bay and the old resort town of Bar Harbor.

This is a land that appeals to the senses, lures one back to the primitive, and inspires the creative minds of poets, artists and photographers. Mount Desert

Island alone is a world unto itself, a world unchanged since the ice left, recycling itself in nature's way and barely touched by man's so-called civilization. Scattered about the island are dozens of lakes and ponds filled with trout, salmon and bass, and surrounded by evergreen forests of balsam fir and red spruce. Wildlife abounds, from the porpoises that glide through the harbors to the white-tailed deer and red fox that roam the forest.

There are other primitive areas here in the east and in the west, but there is something special about Acadia. Some of that, of course, is the geological clock so present. The glaciers departed just a few days ago, relatively speaking, and that sort of tickles the imagination. But there is a moodiness about this place that sets it apart from others. There are times when you can be as alone and remote as any human on earth. When the warm Gulf Stream flowing north in the Atlantic meets the cold Labrador Current just off the coast, moisture condenses into a thick fog that drifts in and envelops the outer islands and the shore of Mount Desert. It closes down fishing and sends vacationers inside; but if you are out along the many trails and pathways in the park, the fog singles you out, isolates you from the world, echoes your thoughts to the innermost soul.

On Acadia it is a time for reflection; the clock stands still as only the roar and crash of the ocean tells of the outside. The rocky shore welcomes the day, then holds it in captivity while man stumbles and ponders and then decides that this is a place of well-being.

Previous pages: an aerial view of the Porcupine Islands in Frenchman Bay, Mount Desert Island. As its name indicates, this bay did indeed once belong to Frenchmen, as the island was the site of a short-lived settlement of French Jesuits in 1613, and for many years was part of the French province of Acadia. Mount Desert Island is of surpassing beauty, a special feature being its breathtaking coastal scenery, such as that near Schooner Head (facing page), and around the Bass Harbor Head Light (above) on the southernmost tip of the island. Acadia's Park Loop Road (right) is particularly attractive in the fall, and encircles the splendid lakeland area below Cadillac Mountain.

Previous pages: Sand Beach, Mount Desert Island. This long, inviting beach is really misnamed, being comprised of tiny shells rather than sand. Nevertheless, edged by the deep green Atlantic and bordered by dark forests of conifers, it remains one of the island's finest walks.

The summit of Cadillac Mountain on Mount Desert Island is the highest point on the Atlantic seaboard of the United States. As a consequence, it is often climbed by visitors (below) eager to witness dawn from the mountain, as the eastern light of morning (left) touches this granite peak before it reaches anywhere else in the country.

Facing page: sunset over Seawall on the south coast of Mount Desert Island. Seawall was named for the unusual natural sea wall that occurs to the north of the town. The town itself contains a ranger station and looks out across the Western Way towards Great Cranberry Island.

Previous pages: a panoramic view of the Bar Harbor area and Frenchman's Bay beyond. Today Bar Harbor is one of the entrances to Acadia National Park, but for many years before the last war it was a society resort. Here many prominent east coast families had their summer homes, and some of their elegant mansions remain today as colleges or inns.

Facing page: sunset beyond Acadia National Park, seen from Mount Cadillac's summit. As it is so high, Mount Cadillac is a natural lookout point for Mount Desert Island and, if the weather permits, a spectacular view of the coast may be enjoyed from here.

Above: wind rustles the birches of Bear Brook, whose fall livery shines bright against the gorge, and (right) exposed rock on the far shore of a Southwest Harbor lake mirrors the white clouds overhead.

Previous pages: a dainty white footbridge leads over a tranquil pond to the Mount Desert Island Museum in Bar Harbor. It is scenes such as this that illustrate why Bar Harbor, and indeed the whole of Mount Desert Island, has been popular with artists since the mid-nineteenth century.

Nearly every landscape in Acadia National Park contains water in some form, and indeed water seems essential to the park's unique beauty. The refreshingly-clean sweep of Sand Beach (above) complements the crystal clear sea at its edge, while this swampy land (left) near Beaver Dam Pond reveals how completely streams dammed by beavers change the landscape of the park. The peace and tranquility of wildernesses, such as the Bass Harbor Marsh (facing page bottom), owe much of their appeal to the rivers running through them, while the wave-racked cliffs below Bass Harbor Head Light (facing page top) make it one of the most romantically-situated lighthouses on the eastern seaboard.

Previous pages: a lone observer on Mount Cadillac, silhouetted against the light of sunrise. This mountain, the highest on Mount Desert Island, often hides its head in the clouds, affording the climber who reaches the summit extraordinary views above the stratus.

The rocky coastline of Mount Desert Island includes some of the highest headlands on the eastern seaboard. Granite is the rock most commonly found strewn on the shore near Schooner Head (above), and sizable boulders can also be seen marking the way on Park Loop Road (facing page top).

Perhaps the finest lake in Acadia National Park is beautiful Eagle Lake (left and facing page bottom). The carriage road around the lake is specially graded for bicycles, and forms part of John D. Rockefeller, Jr.'s legacy to the park. The millionaire financed the island's fifty seven miles of carriage road system.

Previous pages: an aerial view of the eastern coast of Mount Desert Island. One of the best ways to enjoy the magnificent coastal scenery of Acadia National Park is to travel along Ocean Drive, a part of Park Loop Road that is one-way for eleven miles. For the first few miles the drive winds along the eastern slopes of the Champlain Mountains (below), then between Sand Beach and Otter Point it hugs the shoreline, affording dramatic views of the crashing waves below and passing sights such as Thunder Hole and the sheer Otter Cliffs, which rise for 110 feet above the sea.

Left: sunset over a river in Acadia National Park silhouettes some of the many varieties of conifers that cover much of this 44,000-square-mile preserve. Facing page: after a night of thick fog, the mist clears at dawn to reveal Bass Harbor Head Lighthouse in its solitary position at the most southerly tip of Mount Desert Island.

4
Shenandoah National Park

I ain't so crazy about leavin' these hills, but I never believed in bein' agin' the government. I signed the papers they asked me ... I allus said these hills would be the heart of the world.
Hezekiah Lam

Hezekiah Lam was eighty-five the day Franklin D. Roosevelt dedicated Shenandoah National Park. He had lived a long and hard, and no doubt happy and contented, life within the shadows of these Blue Ridge Mountains.

Now, that life had come to an end. Properties had been condemned, families moved. Some went happily, others fought to stay. It was unprecedented, but it was done. "I never believed in bein' agin' the government," Lam had said, but he probably never really understood what it was all about, or, for that matter, Roosevelt's words that day in 1936: "In every part of the country... [we] are engaged in preserving and developing our heritage of natural resources."

The winning back of Shenandoah – winning back rather than saving, for, like the Great Smokies, much of it was already lost – was a long and protracted battle; some forty years in fact if one considers the earliest preservation movements in Virginia.

The impact pre-Europeans made on this land of the Blue Ridge Mountains was negligible, but that native Americans were here as far back as ten thousand years ago is certain. Their burial mounds and artifacts have been found on both sides of the mountains. They fished and hunted and no doubt farmed in some manner. They were Siouan, Monacau, and Manahoacs, and they cleared and burned and they killed for food, but they were small in number and left little sign of destruction. And by the time of the white man, the Indian was gone.

John Lederer, a German, was the first white man to venture into the Blue Ridge. That was 1669. It would be another fifty-five years before settlement would come, but when it came in 1725-1730, it came in full force, and from that day the Shenandoah Valley and the Blue Ridge Mountains were doomed to a sad and untimely demise. By the mid-nineteenth century and the Civil War, the wildlife was gone, the timberland stripped bare, and the precious, thin soil of the mountains eroded to a mere shell.

The valley was settled first, and the farms were successful and profitable, but as more and more pioneers came from eastern Virginia and south from Pennsylvania, land became scarce and families moved up the slopes of the mountains. Soon the forests were gone and the chestnut tree, that marvelous old American chestnut, disappeared. The copper, iron, and manganese miners came and went, and the timber business flourished briefly and then moved on, and the mountain folk, many of whom were totally uneducated, suffered the blight of the whirlwind

As day closes, a pink sky hangs above Big Meadows (above), while at Sawmill Ridge (facing page bottom) a sea of green foliage fades into the distance. Facing page top: the colors of fall contrast with a dusting of snow.

exploitation. The land was unproductive, the scars of the expanding empire bearing mute testimony to a waste of some of *their* most valuable resources.

In the late-nineteenth century a new breed of mountain people came to the Blue Ridge, people who appreciated natural beauty, people who came to play and decry the despoliation. Some of them caught the national park idea from George Freeman Pollock, owner of Skyland Resort and five thousand acres of mountain top, who proposed a preserve here within driving distance of the nation's capital. Although Pollock's preachings were contagious, there was the question of money to buy private land, land owned by families for generations. Virginians, more than twenty-four thousand of them, liked the idea and contributed $1.3 million; the Virginia Legislature added another million and after eleven years of litigation and condemnations, Shenandoah National Park was created.

The forests have taken a long time to recover, indeed they are not fully recovered yet, but this is a splendid three hundred square miles of gentle wilderness where three million people each year renew some faith in nature. They travel the 105 miles of the Skyline Drive, oblivious of the scars still just beyond the roadway and the bitter struggles to provide enough acreage to lend some grace and dignity once again to the old Blue Ridge.

Today, the chestnut fights against the age-old and mysterious disease introduced from Asia in 1900, the disease that finally all but wiped it out, and here and there survives for a few years. Wildlife – not the bison or wolf or elk or the marvelous passenger pigeon who have passed on – is slowly and timidly returning to re-establish a habitat.

It is a new breed of outdoorsmen who now come to the Blue Ridge. This is their one touch of the earth, the rock, the wildflower, the sky. Shenandoah is a "recycled park," once nearly lost and now saved. Its rocks are billions of years old, a foundation of lava flows and crustal upheavals that date to a time when continents shifted and folded and wrinkled. But Shenandoah is also new and bright and warm and friendly. Shenandoah is a re-creation of life that only man in an age of threatened environments can understand and appreciate.

5
Mammoth Cave National Park

It's not much of a house, but we've got one hell of a basement.
Traditional Flint Ridge greeting.
The Longest Cave

Floyd Collins died on February 16, 1925, something of a hero. He did not want it that way, had never planned it that way, but he died with his picture on the front page of newspapers across the country and with his name on the lips of millions of Americans who had never been to Kentucky and who had only the vaguest image of the inside of a cave. Floyd is a legend now, but for 18 days in the winter of '25 he was real – "good copy," as a reporter might say – a press agent's dream.

Floyd Collins was nobody special except to the people of Warren County, Kentucky, who knew him as a cave explorer; an extraordinary caver obsessed with finding a "secret entrance" to the great Mammoth Cave and with making a fortune. In January 1925, Floyd set out to explore Sand Cave on the narrow bridge of land between Flint Ridge and Mammoth Cave Ridge, south of Bowling Green. He was the best in the business and, although he had discovered several caves around there and had commercialized one, Crystal Cave, none of the locations had brought him much money. Rival caves were attracting tourists on their way to Mammoth, but Crystal was too far away. Floyd wanted to be the *first* to catch the visitor's eye; Sand Cave was just right.

Throughout January he dug and scraped and moved rocks and slowly inched his way back through the earth from one passageway to another, each step of the way giving him confidence that soon he would be a rich man. Sometime around the last day of January he was cleaning out a crawlway when a fifty-pound rock fell across his ankle and pinned him to the floor of the cave.

Confident that someone would come to his rescue, Floyd waited. The next morning a friend came, then his brothers, and later his father, himself a caving expert. But Floyd's body filled the crawlway, and no one could get to the rock. It looked bad. By the end of the day the news had gone out that Floyd Collins was trapped in Sand Cave.

News was slow that February 1925, and the Collins story made headlines. The February 2 edition of the *Washington Post* carried a boxed lead: "Man, foot held by rock in cave, is facing death." It shared the front page with a prediction from Secretary of War Curtis Wilbur that a "devastating gas" would wipe out both sides in the next world war. That same day Leonard Sepalla, famed "sleigh musher of the North," was in the final miles of a mercy mission to Nome, Alaska; he was carrying a precious supply of diphtheria serum.

William "Skeets" Miller, a reporter for the Louisville *Courier Journal,* raced to Cave City and

volunteered his services in Floyd's rescue. He was a small man and could fit into tight places and, besides, he wanted the story. Miller immediately began filing his reports, and the Associated Press picked them up and sent them all over the country. For a short time Miller was actually in charge of the operations, moving into tiny openings, talking with Floyd, and helping to move out the debris. By February 4 Miller's name was on the front pages and so was Floyd's picture.

On February 5, Attorney General Harlan Fiske Stone was appointed to the Supreme Court, and a Congressional committee was investigating the "sudden increase in the price of gasoline," but in Cave City, Kentucky, Homer Collins was offering $500 to anyone who could rescue his brother. Another $500 was put up by the crowd that had gathered at Sand Cave. And it was a huge crowd. First came concerned neighbors, then the townspeople, and then people from all over the country. On February 6 the *Washington Post* reported "hundreds," two days later there were "thousands." On the 9th there was a "special to the *Post*" report that 10,000 had collected in the "first real Sunday crowd." Parson Jim Hamilton conducted church services that morning amidst a "country fair atmosphere" that would go on for the next ten days. Hamburgers were twenty-five cents; vendors hawked hot dogs, balloons, apples and soda pop; and there was a three-dollar taxi service to and from town.

"Spectators took a morbid peep at this rock prison," the *Post* said. "After an hour or two of staring, they came back and sat in their flivvers to watch until torch lights lasted into the night." Rumors circulated that first Floyd was rescued and would soon be out, then he was dead, and then that it was all just a publicity stunt for Crystal Cave. It was, of course, much more serious than that, but the Collins family was not above taking advantage of the crowd. During all of this, Floyd's father walked through the crowd passing out leaflets advertising visits to Crystal Cave at "$2 a trip."

The attempts to save Floyd became more daring as time went on. Everyone had a plan, the most promising of which was a shaft drilled from above. Then the ceiling of the cave collapsed and cut Floyd off from all but the engineers on top who frantically pressed down. On the 16th, when the workers finally reached him, Floyd was dead. Newspapers across the nation and in Europe carried banner headlines.

At this point it seemed that nothing could be more bizarre than Floyd's last days, but the events that followed exceeded even the macabre. Floyd wanted to be buried where he fell and his friends complied. The passageway was sealed in concrete. But two months later Floyd's brother, Lee, decided on a proper burial and had the tomb opened. The body was embalmed and reburied near Crystal Cave.

Two years later Lee decided to sell Crystal Cave. Harry Thomas, the man who bought it, had already successfully operated two commercial caves, but Crystal was something special. It was already a drawing card because Floyd Collins had discovered it, but what if – what if Floyd were buried there? Somehow the Collins family agreed. Thomas had Floyd exhumed and placed in the "Grand Canyon," the large entrance room to Crystal, in a glass-covered coffin. Now called "Floyd Collins' Crystal Cave," the newest Cave City attraction was sensational. Thousands filed by Floyd's body while guides told stories about "the world's greatest cave explorer." And there was much more to satisfy the public's morbid curiosity – but that's better left to the public's morbid curiosity.

Overnight, Floyd Collins became the country's most famous caver. The publicity he unwittingly generated was worth millions to this Kentucky valley and, in a sense, he still shares in all that he created. But Floyd is only a small part of the Mammoth Cave story that spans 200 years of written history and probably as much as three thousand years of history known only by archeological findings.

Indians lived in the Mammoth Cave area as early as 1,000 B.C., and there is very good evidence that they knew about the cave and used it; "Lost John," a mummified "miner" discovered in 1935, was digging for gypsum some 2,300 years ago when a huge boulder crushed him to death. Like Floyd Collins, his remains became a tourist attraction until the better senses of the National Park Service put him away.

The first known white man to enter Mammoth Cave was Valentine Simons, in 1798, although he was undoubtedly preceded by many others. Simons bought the land, some two hundred acres, and it was registered in his name at the county courthouse. He mined saltpeter – that's about all the cave was good for in its earliest years – until about 1816 when some travelers began stopping by.

The tourist business did not really begin until the first explorations and mapping in the 1830s, but the cave was still off the "beaten path" and seldom seen. Then, in 1838, Franklin Gorin, who it was said was the first white man born in this region, bought the cave and set one of his slaves, Stephen Bishop, to exploring. Before he died in 1857, Bishop had become America's first great cave explorer. He had seen and mapped more than eight miles of passageways, rooms, streams and rivers, and had gained an international reputation.

What Bishop and his many followers saw was a geological phenomenon quite unlike any in the world, and it attracted the curious from all over, even without the benefit of Floyd Collins. Jenny Lind once gave a concert there, Edwin Booth recited Shakespeare, and even Jesse James held up the old Mammoth stage filled with tourists and relieved them of a few hundred dollars. Today the curious still come to see what water and time have created.

Some 240 million years ago, the seas that covered what is now west-central Kentucky deposited layer-upon-layer of mud, shells, and sand. All of these hardened into the limestone and sandstone we see today. Then, as the land around uplifted, the seas drained away, seeping through cracks in the earth's crust and eroding away the underground stone. Millions of years of this abrasive action created hundreds of caves and passageways and, from the ceilings, where the ground-water has percolated through, myriad colorful stalactites.

One hundred and fifty miles of Mammoth Cave have been explored, and speleologists, that marvelous breed of underground enthusiasts, believe that there may be hundreds more that link this great system to others in this section of the country. The most sought-after and challenging connection was made in 1972, when the Mammoth and nearby Flint Ridge Cave systems were linked by a spunky team of five people who, after a night of some of the most difficult caving, discovered a previously unsurveyed route. It was the top of Everest in the caving world and once again brought Warren County, Kentucky, to the front pages.

"Whether he [Floyd Collins] ever tried to find connections between the big caves does not matter," wrote Roger Brucker and Richard Watson. "He was a caver. He must have thought about it. And the exploration that had led to all the connections in the last twenty years had been made following the footsteps of Floyd Collins."

Mammoth Cave became a national park in 1926 after years of controversy over land acquisitions, and attitudes in these Kentucky hills still reflect the bitter disputes between the federal government and private enterprise. Fortunately for all, nature, at least here, fails to acknowledge man's follies. This is a world unto itself: a room as high as a twenty-story building; delicate, flower-like gypsum crystals; 150 miles of cave on five levels, all spectacular, all inspiring, and preserved for all to enjoy.

Floyd Collins still lies in state in Crystal Cave. Crystal is closed to the public, but no doubt Floyd's spirit explores, wandering endlessly – endlessly.

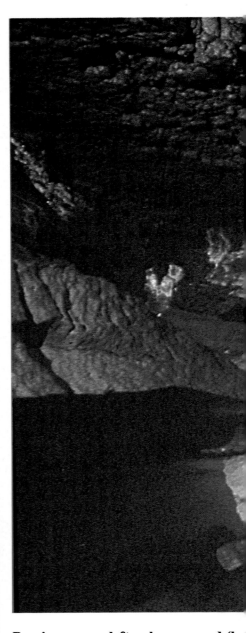

Previous pages left: a beaver, and (be
left) one of the rivers in Mammoth C
National Park where beavers may be
found. The park is noted for its rocks
caves, such as Limestone Bluffs (left),
Roaring River (above), Thorp's Pit
(below) and Kentucky Avenue (right)
(National Park Service Photos).

6

Great Smoky Mountains National Park

We should be impressed by the beauty and fragility of the dynamic balance that has been preserved for so many hundreds of millions of years during which life has persisted on earth. And we should especially appreciate the shortness of our tenure on earth and use the powers we have so recently assumed to perpetuate, not destroy, the balance.
Eliot Porter, *Appalachian Wilderness*

It seems certain now that some of the first humans to inhabit the North American continent passed through the southern Appalachian Mountains. Most likely, too, "they stayed a spell," as today's mountain people might say, for here and there those nomadic tribes of some fifteen thousand years ago left scraps of intriguing evidence. Ethnologists believe they may also have left behind an even greater legacy: one of the largest and most stable of America's early societies, the Cherokee.

If this is true, then the Great Smoky Mountains may be the oldest continuously inhabited area of the country. There was no great drought or violent volcanic eruption to drive this civilization away. They hunted and farmed and thrived in what must surely have been their "Garden of Eden." But, alas, as years went by the Cherokee was nearly destroyed, and *Shaconage,* "the place of the blue smoke," their home for at least a thousand years of recorded time, nearly lost.

The Appalachians are about 400 million years old; that's probably three times older than the Rocky Mountains. There was much earth activity before that and certainly much later, but that seems to be about the time of the "mountain making" in the East. No one knows precisely when the first plants and trees began to root, but it was sometime after the last glacial period. All of that time plotted on the face of a rule stretches nearly to the end. The tragedies of the Smokies came in that last fraction of an inch, between the early 1800s and 1934, when the Great Smoky Mountain National Park was established.

It was the first European settlers who set in motion the chain of events that forecast this land's demise; and it was their descendants who, in the waning hours, wrested it from destruction and saved it.

The Great Smokies are not as delicate as the grassy ocean of the Everglades or as tough as the granite peaks of Yosemite, but like these other great preserves, they have no immunity from the arrogant tools of man. Aldo Leopold wrote: "When some remote ancestor of ours invented the shovel, he became a giver; he could plant a tree. And when the axe was invented, he became a taker; he could chop it down." No doubt the axe came first. It did in the Smokies and sixty percent of this primeval forest fell before natural revegetation began to replenish.

The white man's most dangerous tool, the gun, was the first to enter these mountains, and the Cherokee

Above: a Le Conte Creek waterfall tumbling around massive boulders, and (right) Mingus Mill, in the Great Smoky Mountains' foothills, which once provided ground meal for the early pioneers.

was the first to fall. The Smokies was their home; their first village, Kituwha, was located just inside the present park boundary, near Bryson City, North Carolina. It was these people who named the mountains, and it was they who built a nation long before European influence. Such a culture, however advanced, could offer little resistance against the overwhelming tide of English, Scots-Irish, and German settlers who, following the Revolution, pressed toward the fertile lands of the western frontier. By 1830, their land confiscated, their government voided, and with guns to their backs, the Cherokee succumbed and, in the fall of 1838, in one of the darkest moments of American history, were marched off to what is now Oklahoma.

The Indian had never really tamed this great wilderness, but it was a compatible relationship; he was small in number with few needs for survival and thus made little mark on the land. Not so his conqueror. By the 1850s the valleys and coves had been claimed, fields stripped of rocks and trees, and mountaintops cleared for pasture. Another kind of civilization moved in, and it is still there.

Life in the Smoky Mountains was isolated at first, bare of all but the most essential: a cabin, a spring, oxen for the plow, a few chickens, a cow, if fortunate, and a spinning wheel and rifle. Religion and music became the staples of a simple, unadorned life that forged small communities and knitted several cultures into one. The "mountain people" survived in a world all their own. They liked it that way, and they kept it that way, a private vision of freedom, independence, settlement; a self-sufficient permanence.

These were an exuberant people, courageous and strong and defiant, who could be at the same time generous and violent. They lived hard and they died hard, generation after generation. Life styles changed but little through the years; mail service came, roads linked valleys, and transportation evolved, but customs and traditions clung tenaciously to the hills.

Then, at the turn of the century, the second tragedy of the Smokies began when the Little River Lumber Company bought 8,600 acres of timberland. Systematically, for the next twenty years, the Smokies were mined with no regard for the future. Two-thirds of the forest, trees that had stood for centuries, was cleared to satisfy the insatiable building appetite of the eastern coastal cities. Streams were dammed and then unleashed to carry logs away to the mills; railroads were cut through; mill towns grew; other lumber companies moved in and the industry spread. And with all this, the mountain people changed. They sold their land and their goods and stood by as first the saw and axe and then nature began to turn this once lush, green country, where streams tumbled through the hills and wildlife grazed placidly in the meadows, into a scarred, barren wasteland. Fires jumped from cut to cut; rains washed the unprotected topsoil down and mountains literally slid away, leaving behind the ancient rock. Still, by 1923 there was just enough timber left to make it worth the effort to preserve, in spite of it all, the largest virgin forest in the East.

The beginnings of Great Smoky Mountains National Park is the classic tale of conservation versus industry versus homesteader. It is not a pleasant story, nor can its final chapter ever indicate all that went before. Preservation money was slow in coming, and the well-entrenched families and lumber companies fought the sale of land that continued to yield a living, albeit a sparse one. But private citizens of Tennessee and North Carolina, determined to protect the last vestiges of this wilderness, proposed a national park and fought hard to get it. More than six thousand individual parcels of land comprised the proposed park, and it took millions of dollars and many years of emotionally-charged negotiations to make it a reality. The park was finally established in 1934.

The Great Smokies are a microcosm of the geological and human histories of this nation: the two, man and nature, intertwined in an inexorable struggle against each other. First, the mountains, hundreds of

millions of years of building and sculpturing, and that still goes on as the summers and winters bend and stretch the earth's crust and imperceptibly move things about. Then, man, at first gently and then harshly, altered the landscape and the wildlife that roamed the forest.

But this land belies what has happened. The mountains, seemingly, continue to sleep peacefully, surrounded by that mysterious blue haze that so struck the first Indians. The brilliant display of nature in all its variety and abundance – there are 130 native trees, more than in all of Europe, and more than 1,500 varieties of flowering plants – shields the scars of the past century and deludes the mind. There are more than one-half million acres in the park, and forty percent of it is as it was when the Cherokee first came. The wildlife – nearly dissipated by the time the park was established – is now protected and coming back. There are about 225 species of birds, many on a seasonal basis, 50 species of mammals, 40 of reptiles, and 70 of fish. And, of course, the black bear; that engaging, would-be clown, is the most popular animal in the park. Visitors can drink-in the mountain culture and all the rest that the mountains have to offer, but the one thing they will remember most is the bear.

And the Cherokee is back. (Part of the tribe never left. About a thousand secreted themselves in the most remote areas of the mountains and survived.) The U.S. Government, some years after that terrible "trail of tears" to Oklahoma, permitted the Eastern Band to return and reclaim some of its homeland. Today these proud and patient Cherokee lives on the Qualla Reservation, once again in the shadow of "the place of blue smoke."

The Great Smoky Mountains are a metaphor for nature. The park's 52,000 acres is seventy-five percent wilderness; its 900 miles of trails, 700 miles of streams, and sixteen peaks of over 6,000 feet are a paradise for those who love nature. And they come every year, nearly ten million strong. This is the most visited of all national parks.

Facing page top: the swift-flowing waters of the Oconaluftee River run through the Great Smoky Mountains, flanked by trees colored gold in the fall. These mountains were given the title "smoky" for their appearance in mists and fog, yet even on a clear day they can be veiled in a smoky-blue haze (facing page bottom). Much of this national park is covered by forest, as in the Cherokee Valley area (below), which in earlier times was the home of the great Cherokee Nation and the habitat of wolves, bears and mountain lions. One of the most exciting methods of viewing the forests is by hot air balloon (right). This is a particularly attractive mode of travel in the fall, when varied leaf colors form a patchwork cloak over the hills.

Pioneer settlers in the foothills of the Great Smoky Mountains were both hardy and industrious. They lived simply on small farmsteads (left and facing page), making nearly everything they needed for survival themselves. Old farm implements (left) remain common sights even today, as some mountain people still favor the more traditional methods of cultivating their land. A relic of former times, one of the finest of the pioneer buildings is Mingus Mill (above), also located in the shadow of the Smoky Mountains. Grain would be taken to the mill to be ground, and the miller would be left some of the flour in payment for his provision of this service – an important one upon which the community depended.

Previous pages and right: panoramic views of the Great Smoky Mountains seen from Newfound Gap Road, a route which crosses the border between North Carolina and the neighboring state of Tennessee. The Smokies are formed of some of the highest peaks in eastern North America, as an information board (facing page) high in the mountains illustrates. The Newfound Gap itself exceeds five thousand feet, while Clingman's Dome Observation point, at over a thousand feet higher, affords the visitor a spectacular overlook (below) of the great range.

The Tennessee side of Great Smoky Mountains National Park boasts beautiful waterfalls known as the Sinks (facing page bottom) and Grotto Falls (above). There is a sense of timelessness here that is often found in this park. The mountains themselves contain rocks over a billion years old, and in a few remote coves remnants of the original virgin forest remain, the last of what was once one of the greatest stands of deciduous timber in the world. Over 130 native species of trees grow here, more than in the whole of Europe, and, as might be expected, they are particularly fine in the fall. In fact the valley of Cades Cove (facing page top) and the area known as Chimney Tops (left) are especially rich with color during this season.

Laced with rivers and streams and carpeted with trees, Great Smoky Mountain National Park (these pages) is a living tapestry, threaded with light. Here, myriad leaves, their colors enlivened by the sun, shimmer in the wind, bringing the park alive with movement.

Great Smoky National Park boasts more than eight hundred miles of horse and foot trails, and the woodland scenery (facing page) of the Chimney Tops Trail makes it among the loveliest of these. Rivaling this trail in beauty, however, the Roaring Fork Loop Road winds through the northwest of the park, off which waterfalls (above) form some of the highlights on a fascinating nature walk. The Greenbrier area of the park, near Pitman, also sparkles with clear water (right and overleaf), boasting tranquil lakes and rivers overlooked by a diversity of trees.

Cades Cove (these pages), a large valley lying in the east of the park, is noteworthy for its well-preserved log cabins, such as the Gregg-Cable House (top), Cable Mill (left), Dean Lawson Place (facing page top), and Tipton Place (facing page bottom).

A mountain man once claimed that the Smoky Mountains waterways, such as quaintly-named Little Pigeon River (previous pages), contain the "finest water in this world – clear and sweet year 'round and three degrees colder than ice." Facing page: Morton Overlook, on Newfound Gap Road, presents the traveler with a superb view of the Smoky Mountains. Above: Cable Mill, Cades Cove, one of the many authentic old buildings preserved in this interesting and historic valley, and (right) a sheltered mountain stream beside the Little River Road, in the northwest of the park.

Previous pages: the clear water, soon to be speckled with autumn leaves, of the boulder-strewn Little River in the park's Sugarland Mountain district. In pioneering times this area was covered in sugar maples, hence its name. Facing page: (top) the majesty of the forest-clad Smoky Mountain valleys seen from the summit of Mount Collins, and (bottom) the Little River flowing past a variety of trees cloaked in the many colors of fall at Metcalf Bottoms. Morton Overlook (right), named for one of the national park movement's leaders, gives a long view back down Sugarlands Valley, while the Roaring Fork Motor Nature Trail stretches in a wide, five-mile loop through lush woodland (below).

Left: high summer and (previous pages left) turn of the season beside the Little River. Fall colors generally reach their peak in October in Smoky Mountains National Park, descending the mountains as the season progresses. It is the presence of hardwood species here, such as the red maple and the scarlet oak – usually associated with more northern states – that help to make this such a colorful season in the park. Above: Newfound Gap Road and Sugarland Mountain beyond, as seen from Chimney Tops. The woodland trails to this well-known landmark have to cross numerous streams (facing page and previous pages right). The wider the stream the more light falls through the forest canopy onto it, until such fast-flowing waters can appear as liquid light to the hiker leaving the dim interior of the wood.

Previous pages: Laurel Falls, near Fighting Creek Gap and (right) a brook by the Little River Road. The topography of the Smokies owes much to water erosion, which is responsible for cutting numerous valleys and ravines, clearly visible in an aerial view of the mountains (facing page top) near Clingman's Dome. Around this peak, the highest in the park, the precipitation can amount to eighty-three inches a year and the run-off from such heavy rainfall creates the park's many streams. Clingman's Dome is named for a Civil War general, Thomas Lanier Clingman, who took a special interest in high mountains. For those who share his interest today, this domed mountain is crowned by a magnificent observation tower (facing page bottom). The views from the park's high vantage points are usually spectacular, even at night. Cars winding up the North Carolina side of Newfound Gap Pass (below) create their own beauty as their headlights shine like a moonlit brook in an otherwise dark landscape.

Facing page: Morton Overlook on the
Newfound Gap Road, and (overleaf) one
of the numerous hairpin bends along the
road itself. Despite its high altitude,
Newfound Gap is kept open all year
round by the National Park Service,
though its use is restricted to non-
commercial vehicles. It passes through
both Smoky Mountains National Park
and the Cherokee Indian Reservation on
its way from Asheville to Knoxville,
climbing to an altitude of over 5,000 feet
above sea level as it crosses the state line.

Above: mist drifts across Millikan's
Overlook and Buzzard's Roost and (right)
boulders line the bed of the Little Pigeon
River in the Greenbrier area. Seasonal
mountain floods are normal in the park,
and evidence of such storms of water
remain where the torrent has flung large
rocks high up the river bank.

Facing page: a light cascade of water over Rainbow Falls on the side of Mount Le Conte. The trail to these falls is particularly pretty, lined with an abundance of wild flowers, and boasting some interesting fungi. As the creek itself is shallow for most of the time, its small amount of water almost seems to float over this eighty-foot precipice, thereby creating a fine spray. When sunlight catches this film of water the falls become worthy of their name. Another such hiking trail (right) to Laurel Falls passes through both cove hardwood and pine-oak forest and, as its name would indicate, is rich in mountain laurel. The trail is paved because its popularity with hikers would otherwise lead to its severe erosion, but this does not diminish its beauty. The laurel flowers in late spring, changing large areas of the trail to white or pink, while in mid-summer the purple rhododendron blooms, adding to the advancing tide of color on the walk. Below: a view from Blufton Bridge of the Pigeon River near Hartford and (overleaf) the Little River at Metcalf Bottoms in high summer.

Left: the beautiful reds and golds of fall in the Smoky Mountain Forest, seen from the Laurel Falls Trail. In the past, such forest covered the eastern United States in its entirety – indeed, a squirrel could once have traveled from the Atlantic coast to the Mississippi River without touching the ground. Below: a high, sun-dappled trail near Pitman on a bright autumn day, (overleaf left) Smoky Mountain woodlands in the fall and (overleaf right) a mountain stream beside the trail to Chimney Tops. Facing page top: a distant view of Clingman's Dome from Maloney Point on the Little River Road, where the mountain slopes seem merely shapes of color beyond sparkling green trees. Similarly, the soft light of sunset (facing page bottom) near Morton Overlook reduces the Smokies to simple, overlapping shapes of blue.

7

Hot Springs National Park

The water in the brook was pleasantly tepid, and having no one to intrude upon my privacy, I made a profuse use of it, and wading about found that the hot water came through the slate in an immense number of places...

G.W. Featherstonhaugh, *Excursions Through the Slave States,* 1834

One well-known guide book relegates Hot Springs National Park to its final pages, stating that it barely qualifies for national park status. In comparison to the size and grandeur of Yellowstone and Yosemite and all the others, perhaps the author is right. But the national park concept, as we know it, was developed long after these ancient mineral springs in Arkansas' Ouachita Mountains were set aside by the Congress "for perpetual use and enjoyment of the people." That was in 1832; Yosemite was not discovered for another eighteen years or so. Hot Springs then, in many ways, is our first national park; and if our leaders were slow to apply the same protection policies elsewhere, one can take some small comfort in the knowledge that certain preservation ethics were there in our first century.

It is thought that Hernando de Soto found the springs in 1541. If he did he was probably welcomed by native Americans who had for years used these "miracle" waters as neutral ground, a place where all "miracle" waters could come without warring differences. If not tribes "miracle" waters, at least the Indians considered the forty-some springs to be curative, and things have not changed much in the intervening years.

Hot Springs was rediscovered by the white man when William Dunbar and George Hunter came here in 1804. They collected some samples and, they wrote, "amused ourselves with some further experimental enquiries into the qualities of the hot waters." This brought an end to the quiet time. Within two years settlers had moved in, and the springs have been a going business since.

This was America's spa, at first a group of "wretched looking log cabins," and "a number of baths ... made by hollowing out excavations in the rocks to which hot water is constantly flowing." But as time went on and more and more people came to seek cures for their ailments, the little village flourished. By 1856 there were seven bathhouses and a resident physician. Within another twenty years the town had a population of 3,500 and an annual tourist trade of 50,000. *Harper's New Monthly Magazine,* January 1878, described the hustle and bustle:

"On an autumn afternoon the long straggling street of the town presents a curious picture. On both sides of the thoroughfare, which is half street and half country road, teeming with the variegated

Above and below: the Moorish-inspired buildings lining Bath House Row, (facing page top) the famous color-washed facade of the Arlington Hotel, facing Central Tower across curving Central Avenue, and (facing page bottom) a ranger describing to young guests the fascinating cycle of the thermal water beside a Display Spring, kept open so that visitors can see the water emerging naturally.

population, are ranged a heterogeneous collection of hotels, doctors' offices, stores, saloons, etc., while the bathhouses stretch in long rows on the other side of the creek. Here and there are the country wagons, drawn by gaunt mules or sleepy oxen, passing through the village, halted and bargaining with the hotel or storekeeper for the sale of their load of cotton or produce, or making desperate efforts to get out of the way of the coming horsecars... and everywhere the hogs, in everybody's way and under everybody's feet...'

"It will never be known, I suppose," wrote Freeman Tilden, "just where lies the borderline between the curative powers of the waters and the delightful social experience of exchanging symptoms and other personal history with a similarly minded group." Perhaps that's the charm of this place. Who is to dispute the infirmed who find some marvelous curing quality in this natural phenomenon? They come by the thousands and they bathe by the hour, and they somehow find the magic the Indians knew all along. It's not quite the same now as DeSoto found it, but still the waters flow.

Actually the water is quite hot, an average of 143 degrees Fahrenheit to be exact. And it is old. Old water? That sounds impossible, but the water that bubbles up from these springs - some 850,000 gallons a day - is rainwater that has seeped far into the ground long ago, been heated by the earth's inner core, perhaps - no one really knows - and then been forced to the surface again through a fault in the crust. That round trip can take quite a while. Some parts of the water have been determined twenty years old, while other parts are 4,000 years old. If this is true, then some of the springs are now issuing water many times the age of the trees and plants that surround this 6,000-acre park. Like seeing the glacial parks of the North and West, a walk through the Ouachita woodland makes man seem small, almost infinitesimal, in the overall plans of nature. Hot Springs National Park is a restful place. It was to the Indian; it is again to his inheritor.

Since its beginnings in the early 19th century, the town of Hot Springs, in the center of Hot Springs National Park, has grown from being a group of "wretched-looking log cabins" to become one of the most elegant spas in the country. The Bath House (top and top right) and the Arlington Hotel (above) are two examples of such elegance in architecture, while banks of azaleas in the Woodland and redbuds and dogweed (right) on Whittington Avenue are indicative of the town's beautiful setting.

8
Virgin Islands National Park

Three miles westward from St. Thomas, across the flashing blue waters of Pillsbury Sound, lies St. John, the smallest, most romantic and best-beloved of the Virgin Isles. … It is as wild, detached and primitive as if it were lost somewhere on the rim of an unknown sea.
Hamilton Cochran

This nation has been inordinately fortunate in real estate investments. If you consider the twenty-four dollars for Manhattan a valid sale, it was a good deal. No less so was Thomas Jefferson's crafty and secret purchase of the Louisiana Territory from Napoleon in 1803 for $16 million; the territory included one-third of the United States. And there was "Seward's folly" – Alaska. In 1867, Secretary of State William H. Seward negotiated the purchase of Alaska from Russia for $7.2 million. Both the Louisiana and Alaska deals were questioned at the time, but Jefferson and Seward have long since been vindicated.

In 1803 it seemed, at least to President Jefferson, that the security of the United States was in jeopardy when Napoleon sent French troops to quell a rebellion in Santa Domingo. Suspecting that this might be a launching base for invasion, Jefferson took advantage of time and made Napoleon an offer. It was accepted.

Similarly, in 1917, fearing that Germany had its eye on the Danish-owned Virgin Islands in the Caribbean as a naval base, the United States made another real estate deal. For $25 million we bought the three largest islands, St. Thomas, St. Croix, and St. John, and approximately fifty small islets and cays. Whether or not this altered the war in the Atlantic is questionable but, following hostilities, the purchase caused considerable debate. That was a lot of money for a group of seemingly useless islands 900 miles off shore. It was hailed as another "Seward's folly." But as with the Alaska investment, time vindicated all involved. It turned out to be a bargain.

Columbus discovered these tropical islands on his second voyage in 1493 but, as seemed his luck, he was not the first; South American Indians had been there since 300 A.D. Their village remains and petroglyphs have been found scattered about St. John.

Although there were various claims on the islands during the next two hundred years, St. Thomas and St. John were not formally settled until the early eighteenth century and then by private, chartered companies that established sugar and cotton plantations. The Danes were the first on St. John in 1718. Within a short time they had built mills and roads and imported slaves from West Africa, but neither sugar nor cotton were suited to the islands and the industries were never really successful. The slaves rebelled in 1733. Production dropped significantly and prosperity waned until, in 1848, emancipation was proclaimed by the Danish Governor, to prevent what was believed to be a major revolt. The plantation era soon ended, but the island had been virtually stripped of its native growth and wildlife.

By the time the United States took possession in 1917, some attempts were being made to reintroduce native plants and animals. Of course, by now nature has reclaimed much of the land. Evidence of the previous occupation is most noticeable in the ruins of the Danish industries. More than eighty separate estates operated at one time or another. The remains of the Annaberg, Cinnamon Bay, and Reef Bay plantations are particularly significant, and while subject to the whims of the jungle, they remain as vivid and picturesque reminders of the island's past.

Interest in setting aside the entire island of St. John as a national park began in the early 1950's with the rapid growth of tourism and commercial development on nearby St. Thomas. Word had spread about this little, out-of-the-way place called St. John: white beaches, mountains rising 1,200 feet, and a year-round average temperature of 78 degrees. Only a few miles from St. Thomas, and forty miles from St. Croix, it was virtually inaccessible, so few got here to vacation. One who did, however, was Laurence Rockefeller, who contributed five thousand acres of privately-owned land to the federal government. Additional land was acquired, and on August 2, 1956, Virgin Islands National Park was established. Other acreage has been acquired in recent years to enlarge the park, but it is not likely that the island itself will ever be completely within the park boundaries. St. John is only nine miles long and five miles wide; the park includes about three-quarters.

The Virgin Islands are the tips of ancient sedimentary deposits and were formed in much the same way as other areas in the national parks. Even here the theories of plate tectonics and the moving of the earth's crust over explosive funnels in the core beneath explains much of the land construction. What all of this has left us is a priceless tropical island of sparkling bays, brilliant beaches, and forested mountains and valleys.

Virgin Islands National Park is on what some call the heavenly side of St. John, where the trade winds and sparkling waters bring fantasies of pirates and buccaneers, where man's conflict with nature is washed fresh by the unspoiled sea, and where the solitude of a visit renews one's communication with the outside world.

Previous pages: right (top) Trunk Bay, and (bottom) coral reefs at Leinster Bay, Virgin Islands National Park. The forest was once cleared for farmland, but it has now regrown and, where the trees meet the shore by Europa Bay (facing page) and Cinnamon Bay (top and right), it is very beautiful. Above: dildo cactus in a forest clearing on the island.

9

Everglades National Park

*I somehow feel sure … that what does remain of the Everglades will always be there, for how much poorer America
would be without it.*
Michael Frome, *The National Parks*

No other natural area in the National Park System, and perhaps the whole of the United States, is so delicately balanced between survival and destruction as the Everglades of Florida. And yet it has been abused by man and man's follies more than any other. Some speculate that if we ever lose a national park, it will probably be the Everglades. Not through development – the boundaries are firmly fixed and the land protected from the bulldozer forever – but from the steady tipping of the ecological scales.

The Everglades is a broad, flat river of fresh water that flows from Lake Okeechobee in central Florida 120 miles south to Florida Bay and the Gulf of Mexico. It has done so since time unknown; an endless "river of grass" that moves so imperceptibly that it seems to stand still. The life it once cradled and nourished may have been the most abundant anywhere, an incredible array of nature which, even before man came to Florida, clung tenaciously to a shallow foothold.

Southern Florida is low country; the highest point in the state, in the northern panhandle, is only 345 feet above sea level. Here in the Everglades land height is measured in inches. It was not always like this. Several times in the past million or so years, it seems, the sea level between glacial periods left this peninsula of ancient limestone high and dry. As glaciers melted, the sea rose and the land was once again covered. During these remote periods ridges of limestone were built along the outer perimeters of the now Florida shape, thus creating a shallow bowl effect.

This was the setting for the creation of the Everglades – a limestone basin, tilted slightly to the south and west, and lined with layers of peat, decayed grass and marsh plants, which collected the abundant summer rainfall (about sixty inches a year) and set it flowing, gently, to the sea.

Essentially this is what the Everglades is today, except some changes have been made that for the past seventy years have seriously jeopardized the existence of this subtropical wonderland. And the cause of these changes? Why, man, of course!

Both coasts of Florida were inhabited by Indians when explorers arrived in the early 1500s. Some say they were descendants of the ancient civilizations of Mexico and Peru. Whatever they were, by the late eighteenth century they had disappeared, leaving behind only their burial mounds as evidence of their tribes. During the early-1800s purge of the Creek Confederation in the southern states, many from these tribes took refuge in the Florida Everglades and

became known as the Seminoles. Even here they were not beyond the arm of military pursuers, but they survived and have lived quietly and unobtrusively, and nearly forgotten, since.

The white man "discovered" Florida around the turn of the century. One of his "discoveries" was that by drawing water from the Everglades, the resulting soil, thin as it was, could be farmed. Dikes were laid around Lake Okeechobee, canals were built and fresh water let to the sea. Miami was founded on the east coast, and the race was on. But somewhere along the way the developers met themselves coming around the bend. Okeechobee flooded and spilled and thousands died; the fine, organic soil oxidized and the peat base burned; salt water filtered in to fill the fresh

Willowhead freshwater slough on the Anhinga Trail (below) and the Tamiami Trail's mangrove swamp (facing page) are among the many beauties of the Everglades.

water vacuum, and the Everglades began to dry up in the drought season – wildlife and plants and trees with it. The whole fragile ecological system of southern Florida had been turned upside down. It was a disaster!

One of the key factors in upsetting nature's balance in the Everglades, and, oddly enough, the same in spurring preservation movements, was, like beaver-trapping in the northwest, the fashion industry. Some of the early Florida settlers found that around 1886 there was a very profitable market in the plumes of tropical birds, primarily the herons and snowy and great egrets. The New York millinery industry paid handsome prices for these feathers, and the Everglades was a forest of herons and egrets. Almost overnight business boomed. Hunters galore pursued nesting places with a vengeance, until by 1905 game wardens were being murdered and the herons and egrets had all but disappeared.

The Audubon Society stepped in to protect the birds. It was followed by other conservation organizations which sought just to preserve what was left of the rapidly diminishing ecological system. By 1916 a small section of the Everglades was set aside as a state park. Congress authorized Everglades National Park in 1934; it was formally established in 1947.

Only one-seventh of the Everglades is within park boundaries, about 1.4 million acres, and though it is still besieged on all sides by man-made water problems, its legislated borders have given time; precious time in a struggle for survival.

The Everglades is a certain kind of magic. Both ugly and beautiful, this magic – a sense of mystery and discovery – transcends the absolutes, the complexities, the disjointed and calamitous events that nearly destroyed and still threaten. Here is a tropical life blended with the temperate climate zone, where the nature of the mid-Atlantic states meets the species of the Caribbean in a rare setting of conflicts and contrasts.

The once endangered alligator is now making a comeback; fifty pairs of southern bald eagles balance somewhat tenuously on the endangered species list; the Florida panther (cougar) may not make it another century. Some birds and mammals will never be seen again in the Everglades. For them the boundaries have come too late.

Life in the Everglades hangs by a tiny thread. Man's progress, the constantly growing cities, his persistent invasion of nature's sanctuary – all of this tugs at one end, while at the other the delicate web dangles, patiently waiting.

Everglades National Park is a refuge – it can be a refuge for man if he only stops and tries to understand.

Facing page: a young alligator basks on a branch in the Florida sun and (below) cypress trees reach high above their swamp-grown roots.

Top: a stand of slash pines lining open water in Big Cypress Swamp. Left: new vegetation quickly reclaims ground cleared by a burn, and (above) waterweed floats on the surface of a freshwater pond. Among the species that flourish in such environments are the tiny-leaved duckweed, watermeal or wolffia and the floating fern or azolla. Facing page: (top) cabbage palms, and (bottom) mangrove forest along the saltwater coastal fringe of Big Cypress Swamp. Overleaf: great egrets and a wood stork feed among water lettuce, a free-floating plant which virtually covers many lakes in Corkscrew Swamp.

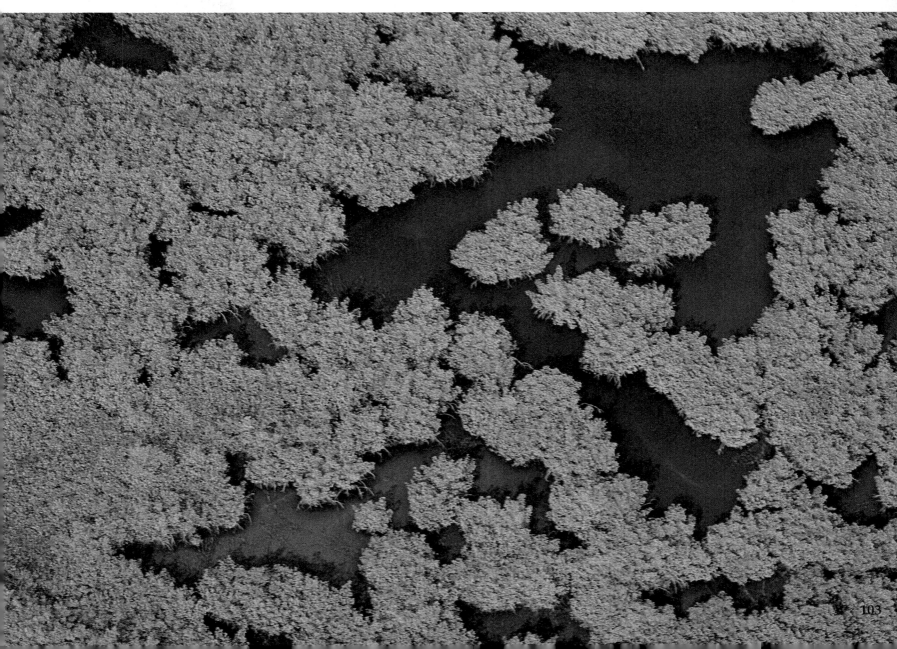

The anhinga's distinctive plumage (right) can become so sodden during the underwater stalking of its prey that it cannot fly, and has to clamber and claw its way to a safe perch. Facing page: an anhinga preening, and (bottom) an anhinga with back feathers fluffed, wings outstretched and tail fanned to dry. Below: an immature great blue heron. Overleaf: an airboat skims across water lettuce, piloted by a Miccosukee Indian guide.

Madeira Bay (facing page) lies east of Flamingo on the north shore of Florida Bay. Right: a brown pelican in summer plumage, and (below) the white variant of the great blue heron, found only in salt water from southern Biscayne Bay around the coast to Everglades City. Discovered by John James Audubon, the great white heron will breed with the great blue, and the two birds are now considered to be of the same species.

The old road (left) to Flamingo, now traveled only on foot, is being fast encroached upon by the surrounding forest. Below: sunset over prairieland of sawgrass and dwarf cypresses. A site adaptation of the variant known as pond cypress, these low trees are stunted by poor, thin soil and fluctuating water levels. Bottom: wild pine, an epiphyte member of the pineapple family.

Raccoons (these pages) hunt, forage and scavenge for a wide variety of foods, including fish, oysters, insects, small mammals, birds and their eggs, and many fruits and plants. With the onset of the dry season in November their abundant food supplies are drastically reduced and, together with their prey and predators, they search the dried-up prairies even for water. By the time the first spring rains come, in about May, many have died of thirst and starvation. Overleaf: Shark River Slough, set with dense hammocks of tropical hardwood trees and alive with alligators.

Facing page: (top) a great blue heron stands motionless and ready to strike (bottom). Left: red and green bracts on the flower stalk of the wild pine, a bromeliad which usually grows in the bark of the cypress. The Anhinga Trail (top) passes over Taylor Slough (above), a slow-moving, freshwater, marshy river. On a smaller scale, sloughs form where water gathers in shallow troughs in the limestone bedrock, and may retain much-needed water even into the winter dry season.

Both natural and manmade fires (facing page and below) played a major role in shaping the Everglades. The Seminole Indians burned the prairies to flush out game, to kill ticks and rattlesnakes, or to make new grazing for their cattle and ponies. The white ranchers who displaced them continued the practice. Fire is now employed to conserve the landscape rather than change it; for example, at Corkscrew Swamp controlled burning is used to stop the encroachment of the coastal willow onto the central marsh. Right: ragwort flourishes on land cleared by a burn at Corkscrew Swamp. Bottom: dwarf cypresses and sawgrass.

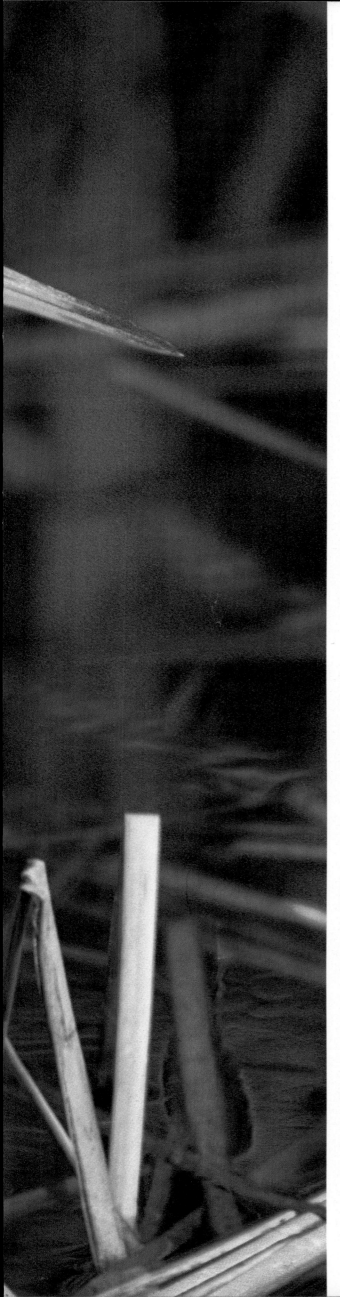

The offspring of the largest of North American herons, an immature great blue heron (bottom) may grow to an adult height of four feet. The Louisiana heron (left) feeds along saltwater shores, in company with the white ibis (below). White ibis often congregate in large flocks, flying in long lines or in V-formation. Different types of heron and other water birds will readily share both feeding and nesting grounds, and noisy, untidy mixed rookeries are a distinctive feature of cypress and mangrove forests.

Facing page: (bottom) evening on Lake Trafford, near Immokalee in Big Cypress Swamp (top). Top: a stand of slash pines and the blue spikes of pickerelweed lining slow-moving freshwater near Immokalee. Left: a great blue heron among overhanging willow, and (above) an alligator.

125

The raccoon flourishes in almost every habitat to be found in the Everglades. Bottom right: hunting warily in Corkscrew Swamp Sanctuary. Right and bottom: alligators emerge from the water to sun themselves, thus raising their externally-controlled body temperature. Below and bottom: dense surface coverings of water lettuce, a major source of the dead vegetation continually being laid down as a rich, organic peat. Overleaf: sunset over Key Largo.

This page: roseate spoonbills feeding in the saltwater shallows of the coastal Everglades. The spoonbill's distinctive, flattened bill provides it with a broad area through which to sift mud and water for the small marine life on which it feeds. Facing page: (top) a freshwater pond in Taylor Slough, on the Anhinga Trail, where (bottom) a common moorhen feeds on aquatic vegetation and pondlife.

Alligators (these pages) mate in April and May, during which time the bulls will fight (facing page bottom). The female builds a nest of weeds and rotting leaves, raised into a mound above the water, where she lays up to 60 eggs in late May or June. Incubated by the heat of the sun and the decomposing vegetation, the eggs hatch after about 65 days to release miniature alligators about nine inches long. Below: young alligators. Overleaf: Ten Thousand Islands, off Florida's west coast.

Slider turtles (bottom right) dig themselves into the moist undersoil at the onset of the dry season, and there survive the drought in a state of aestivation – a condition akin to hibernation, but not as deep or sustained. During particularly severe drought even the reservoir-like 'gator holes may prove insufficient, and alligators (remaining pictures) will aestivate in damp dens adjoining their dried-up waterholes.

Above: a Louisiana heron, generally found on saltwater shores, and (far right center) a green heron, shorter necked than most types of heron. Top far right: an alligator waits, almost entirely submerged, for unwary prey. Top: canoeing, and (right) a tangle of red mangrove roots on the upper Turner River, near Chokoloskee.

Corkscrew Swamp Sanctuary (these pages) was established with the aid of the National Audubon Society, which is now responsible for the conservation and management of the area. To protect both swamp and visitors the Society constructed a boardwalk extending for more than a mile – over ponds covered with water lettuce (facing page and above), wet prairie (top), and past air plants growing thickly on the trunks of bald cypresses (right). Broad buttresses, which can grow to be eight to ten feet across, help the cypress trees' shallow root systems to support their height in unstable ground.

141

Facing page top: red mangroves grow in shallow salt water at Ten Thousand Islands, supported on curved prop roots. The stems of the saw palmetto (facing page bottom) are short, reclining trunks supporting many leaf bases, from which grow stiff, divided leaves. Right: charred saw palmettos, and (bottom) burnt woodland of saw palmettos and slash pines. The moist bark of pines and palmettos gives them a degree of resistance to fire, and they can recover quickly following limited burns. Below: shoveler ducks and double-crested cormorants. Overleaf: an ahinga spreads its wings to dry.